W9-AMP-845

Sports Illustrated KIDS

WHOOSH, CRUNCH, ROAR

FOOTBALL ONOMATOPOEIA

By Mark Weakland

CAPSTONE PRESS
a capstone imprint

Grunt! Whap! Whoa! Sounds of action and excitement fill a football game. Today's game features **onomatopoeia**, words that sound like the things they describe. Let's get in the game and look for football onomatopoeia. Wow!

Onomatopoeia can describe the speed of a quarterback's pass. He steps forward and fires the ball. **Whiz!** The football **zooms** through the air like a bullet. If the pass is on target, the ball will **zip** into the hands of an eager receiver.

The holder takes the snap from the center. He **plunks** the ball down on the turf. **Bam!** The kicker launches the ball high into the air. When he lifts his head, he hopes to see the football sail through the goalpost uprights.

Crunch! Onomatopoeia sometimes sounds hard. Pads and helmets **clack** and **clatter** as defensive players fall upon a lone receiver. But don't worry! Football players are strong and sturdy. This one's tough enough to survive a football player pyramid.

The **hum** of the crowd turns to louder cheers and chants. Fun-loving fans begin to wave their arms and yell. Soon the noise becomes a wild **roar**. This onomatopoeia sounds loud. All the thunder and racket from the stands makes playing difficult for the visiting team.

A defensive player launches himself at a running back. **Wham!** He crashes into the back's chest pads. **Oof!** Onomatopoeia can really pack a wallop! If the ball carrier doesn't hold on tightly, a hard hit can make the ball pop out.

Tweet! Onomatopoeia describes the high **warble** of a ref's whistle. A shrill **trill** from the referee signals a safety. That's two points for the defensive team, and they get the ball back. What a game changer!

At the line of scrimmage, bodies collide with a **thump** and a **thwack**. **Thud, thud!** That's the sound of players' feet **tromping** across the turf as they push for position. If the defensive linemen can force their way into the backfield, they just might sack the quarterback.

Squirt! A thirsty player squeezes a stream of water into his mouth. **Ahh!** The sound of onomatopoeia has never been so refreshing. Because players lose water through sweating, they drink lots of liquids during the game. After a long swig, this lineman is ready to get back in the game.

Onomatopoeia helps describe the muddy mess of playing on a rain-soaked football field. **Squish!** Mud oozes up and over the shoes of straining players. **Splat!** Soggy linemen fall as they struggle to tackle the running back.

The joy and fun football players feel during the game can be found in onomatopoeia. Players **snicker**, **snort**, and **chortle** as they goof around. And when someone says something really funny, you'll hear a loud **guffaw**. Ha, ha!

What is the sound of victory? **Whoosh!** Players gleefully dump a bucket of water and ice over their coach. For teams that win a championship, this ritual is a fun—and cold—way to celebrate. **Sploosh!** Would you like to be the coach or the players?

Teams also celebrate a big win with fireworks. Rockets sizzle as they streak upward, leaving silvery trails. Then **pop**, **boom**, **bang!** Explosions of orange and red light up the night.

In an action-packed game, football sounds are everywhere. Can you find the onomatopoeia used to describe the action in this play?

Two defenders turn with a grunt, too late to stop a pass that thuds into the chest of a leaping receiver. The crowd buzzes with excitement as cameras click to capture the action. Wow, what a catch!

Answer: grunt, thuds, buzzes, click, wow

GLOSSARY

boom (BOOM)—a deep, prolonged sound

clatter (KLAT-ur)—a loud, rattling sound; the sound created when two things crash together

hum (HUHM)—a low, continuous buzzing sound

onomatopoeia (on-uh-mat-uh-PEE-uh)—the formation of a word based on a sound

sizzle (SIZ-uhl)—to make a hissing sound

squirt (SKWURT)—to shoot a liquid out quickly

thud (THUHD)—a dull sound from a heavy step or blow

tweet (TWEET)—a shrill, high-pitched sound from a bird or whistle

warble (WAR-buhl)—a whistle sound that changes pitches

whiz (WIZ)—to move very fast, often with a humming or buzzing sound

zoom (ZOOM)—to run or move quickly

READ MORE

Blaisdell, Bette. *A Mouthful of Onomatopoeia*. Words I Know. North Mankato, Minn.: Capstone Press, 2014.

Rosen, Michael. *We're Going on a Bear Hunt*. Somerville, Mass.: Candlewick Press, 2014.

Speed Shaskan, Trisha. *If You Were Onomatopoeia*. Word Fun. North Mankato, Minn.: Capstone Press, 2008.

INTERNET SITES

FactHound offers a safe, fun way to find Internet sites related to this book. All of the sites on FactHound have been researched by our staff.

Here's all you do:

Visit *www.facthound.com*

Type in this code: 9781620651605

INDEX

Sports Illustrated Kids Football Words are published by Capstone Press,
1710 Roe Crest Drive, North Mankato, Minnesota 56003
www.capstonepub.com

Library of Congress Cataloging-in-Publication Data
Cataloging-in-Publication data is on file with the Library of Congress.
ISBN 978-1-62065-160-5 (library binding)
ISBN 978-1-4914-7600-0 (eBook PDF)

Editorial Credits
Anthony Wacholtz, editor; Terri Poburka and Ted Williams, designers;
Eric Gohl, media researcher; Katy LaVigne, production specialist

Photo Credits
Newscom: MCT/Sam Riche, 22–23, ZUMA Press/Tim Warner, cover, 1; Sports Illustrated: Al Tielemans, 6–7, 10–11, Bill Frakes, 14–15, Bob Rosato, 20–21, Damian Strohmeyer, 24–25, David E. Klutho, 2–3, 8–9, 12–13, 16–17, 28–29, John W. McDonough, 26–27, Simon Bruty, 4–5, 18–19

Design Elements: Shutterstock

Printed in the United States of America in North Mankato, Minnesota.
032015   008823CGF15